Dedicated to Stephanie

This is a book about ballet...

A career you might want to choose...

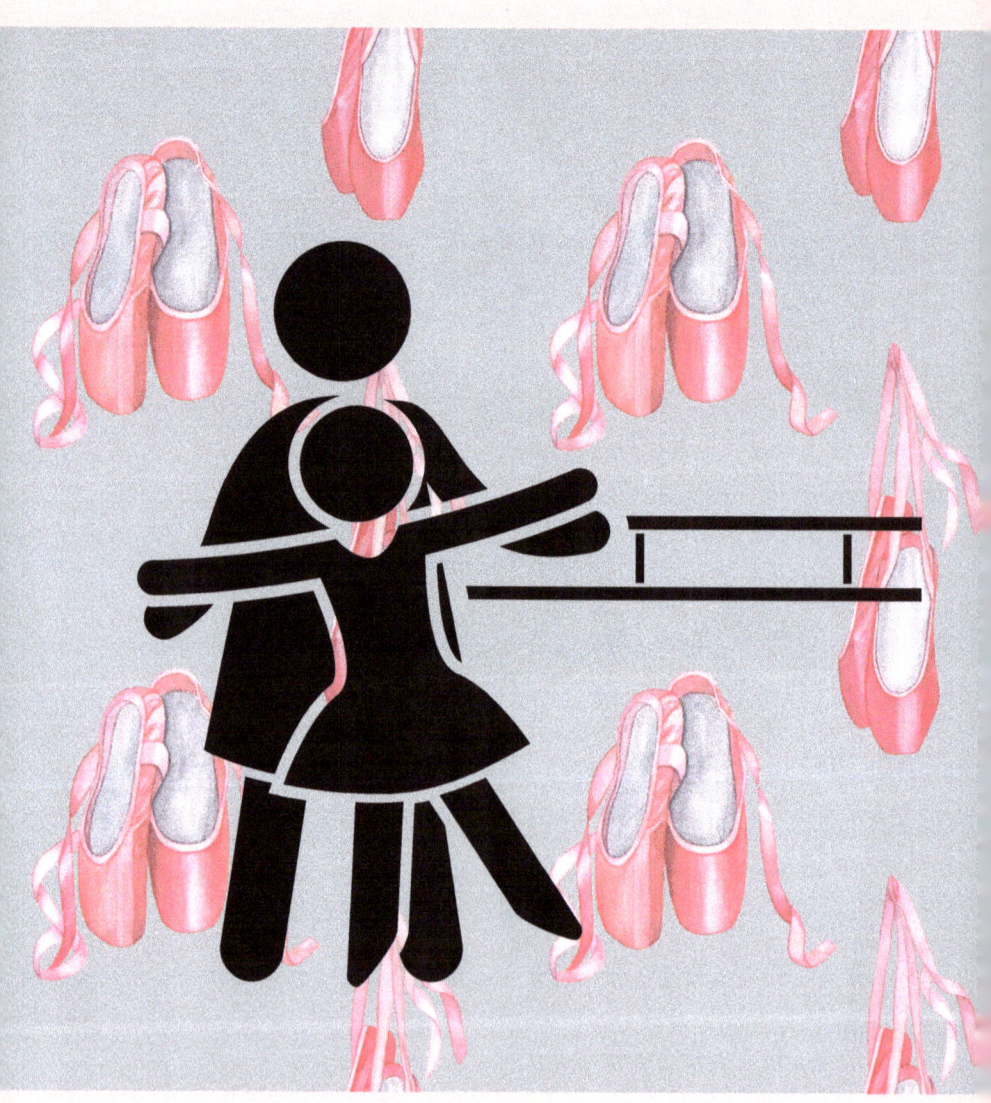

If you'd like to be a professional ballet dancer...

And wear a pink tutu!

If you're a girl you could be a Ballerina...

If you are a boy you could be a Ballerino.

It takes a lot of hard work to be a ballet dancer...

10+ years of training. A commitment that will only grow.

First you must learn proper posture...

Body alignment...

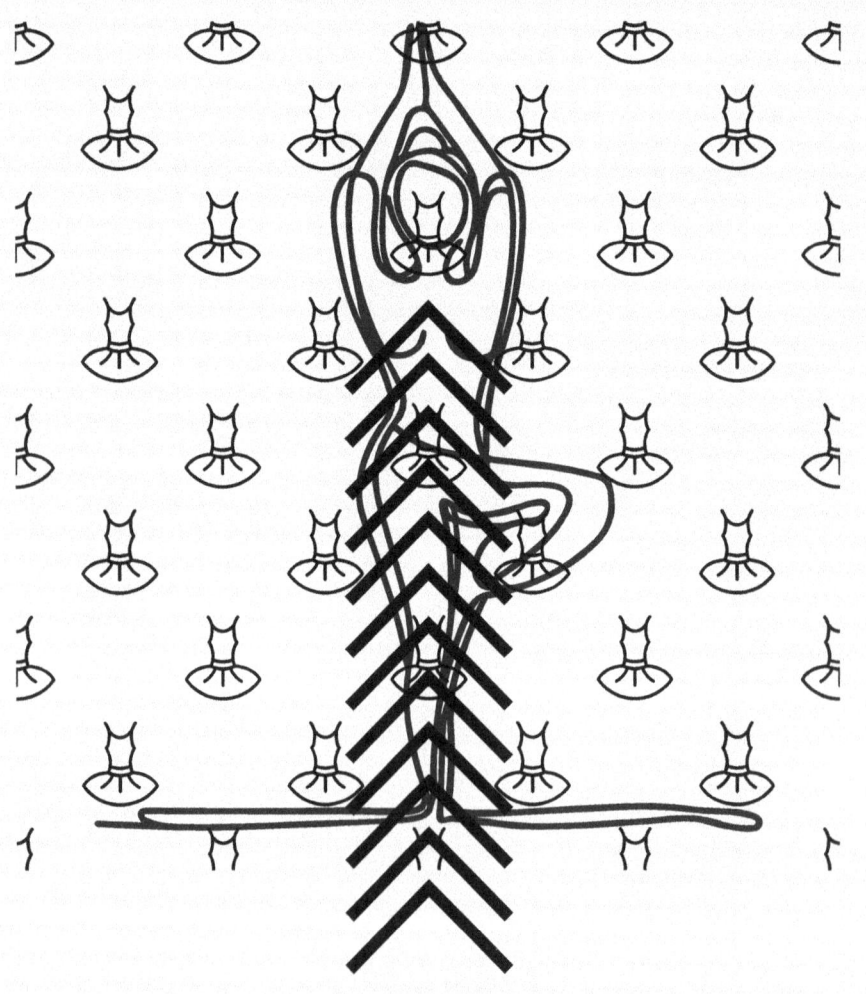

And coordination.

There's so much to learn and so much to do...

You have to decide if it's the right career for you.

It's difficult enough to learn skills in ballet...

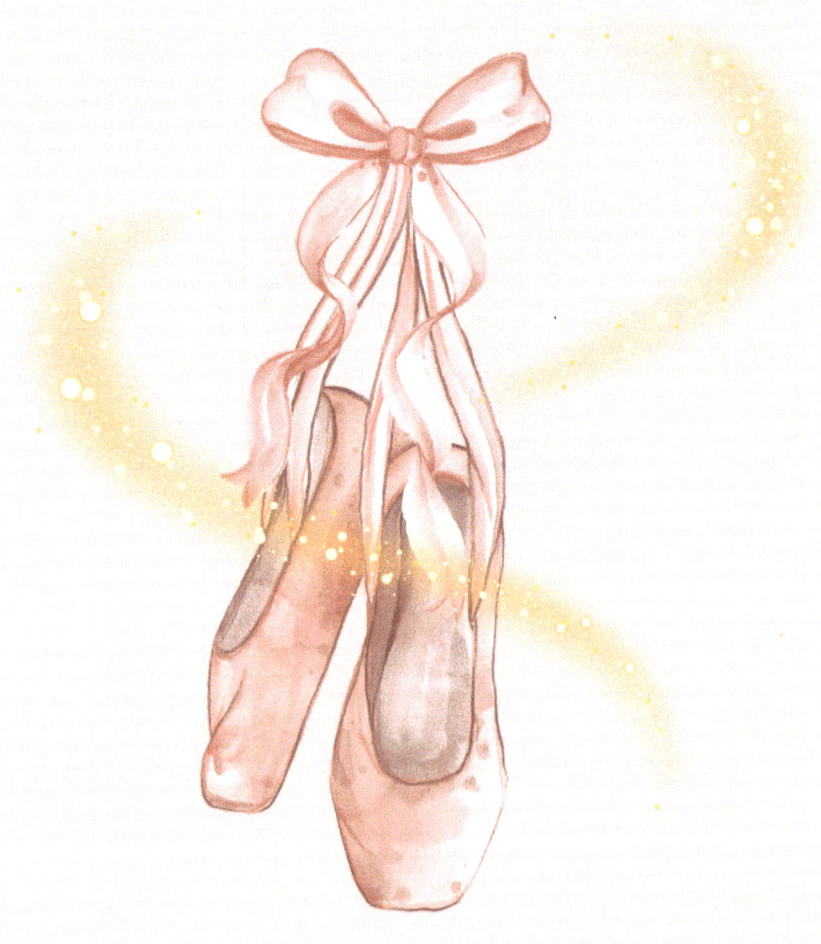

Even with the best of teachers...

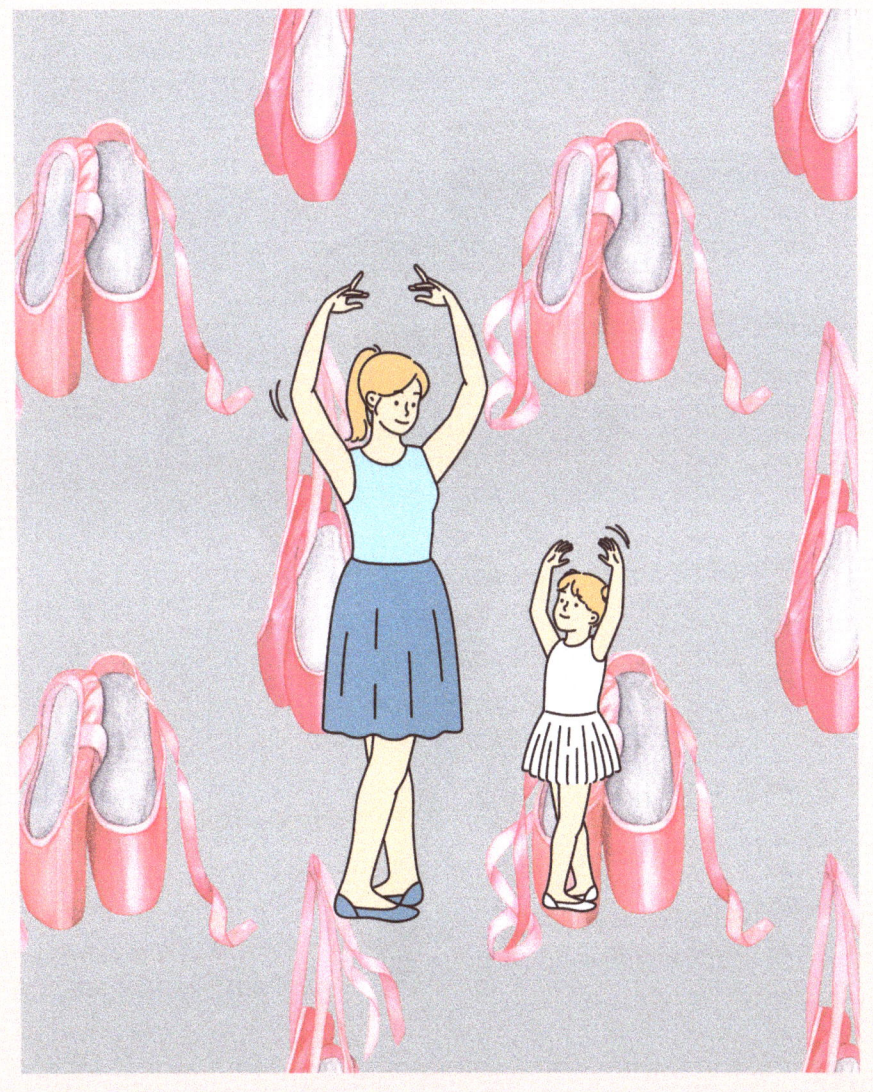

Who knew I'd be able to JUMP JUMP JUMP for the debut...

Of a MOO-MOO
in a tutu!"

To be a ballerina you need strong legs ankles and toes...

And walk softly as ballerinas do...

So, it would be fun being a ballerina or ballerino...

It's good to have a plan and now it's time to...

JUMP JUMP JUMP

For the debut of the MOO-MOO in a tutu!

WE

moo-moos
in tutus!

Jump Series:

Jump Like a Caribou!
Jump Like a Kangaroo!
Jump at the Zoo!
Jump and Say P.U.!
Jump and Say Boo!
Jump and Say Valentine's Day Is
For Kids Too!
Jump and Look For a Clue!
Jump and Say Happy Birthday to You!
Jump For Everything Blue!
Jump, Hop and Say Happy Easter To
You!
Jump and Say Cock-A-Doodle-Do!
Jump and Sing Da-Do-Do-Do!
Jump and Ask Who? Who?
Jump and Squawk Like a Cockatoo!
Jump and Ask Is It You or Ewe?
Jump and Say There's an Ewww in My
Stew!
Jump and Say Merry Christmas To You!
Jump and Cheer Happy New Year!
Jump and Say There's a Hare in My
Hair!

Jump and Say My Aunt Ate An Ant!
Jump and Say There's An Aardvark In
The Amusement Park!
Jump and Buzz Like A Bee!

Clap For Series
Clap for 1!
Clap for 2!
Clap for 3!
Clap for 4!
Clap for 5!
Clap for 6!
Clap for 7!
Clap for 8!
Clap for 9!
Clap for 10!

The Cat Who Said Hello
The Three Boulders
Billy Shakespeare
Billie Shakespeare
Learn To Draw With Symmetry
ABC More Learn to Draw With Symmetry

Non-Fiction
103 Fundraising Ideas For Parent Volunteers With
Schools and Teams